REMEMBERING TWO BAPTIST PIONEER PREACHERS OF TEXAS

Original Book Released in 1939 by
Della Tyler Key
Entitled
*Two Baptist Pioneer
Preachers of Texas
and their Genealogy*

Updated Edition by
Sidney F. Alford

Remembering Two Baptist Pioneer Preachers of Texas

© 2009 by Sidney F. Alford

Published by Dennis Bros. Printers, Inc.
2313 19th Street
Lubbock, Texas 79401

Printed in the United States of America

Edited by Judy Bowyer, *Write to your Heart,* Petersburg, Texas

Cover design and layout by Judy Bowyer

All rights reserved. No part of this publication may be reproduced, stored in a retrieval system, or transmitted in any way by any means, electronic, mechanical, photographic (photocopying), recording, or otherwise, without the prior permission of the publisher, except as provided by United States copyright law.

ISBN 978-0-615-29790-3

ACKNOWLEDGEMENTS

Many thanks to the kind people at the Bethel Church for their helpfulness and their good directions to the cemetery, and for providing the original minutes from the Bethel Church.

Thank you to the people in Carthage at the Panola County Historical Society for supplying additional historical information.

And my thanks to Judy Bowyer, long-time family friend, for her design and formatting assistance in putting together this book.

To order copies of this book, contact:

Sidney F. Alford
PO Box 772
Petersburg, TX 79250
Email: sfalford@gmail.com

TABLE OF CONTENTS

Acknowledgements 3

Table of Contents 5

Preface 7

Chapter 1 . . . . Original Material from Della Tyler Key 9

Chapter 2 . . . . Reed Genealogy compiled by Della Tyler Key 32

Chapter 3 . . . . Reference Information from Key's book 38

Chapter 4 . . . . Additional Material from Sidney Alford 39

Endnotes 40

Chapter 5 . . . . Photos 41

Index of Main Events 48

PREFACE

The original volume of Two Baptist Pioneer Preachers of Texas and Their Genealogy was printed in 1939 by Della Tyler Key.

I first read about Issac Reed in 1992. Reed was my great-great-great-great grandfather and Della Tyler Key was a cousin. My intent is to remain true to her original published work; therefore I have included the contents of her book virtually verbatim, with only a few typographical or grammatical changes. To further enhance the work, however, I have added extra material and my own photographs, taken at the church sites and gravesites mentioned in the original book.

Everyone should read and learn the history of our country. In 1820, when Texas was opened to Anglo-American immigration, the state religion was Roman Catholic [according to facts from the Texas Almanac 2008-2009].[1] All who moved to Texas were required to embrace the Catholic religion, and the practice of other religions was prohibited. So when Issac Reed arrived in 1834, he was faced with impending consequences if he practiced or introduced Protestant teachings. At times fearing for his life, Issac Reed went about the vicinity, teaching and preaching privately.

We all need to pray that no minister of the Gospel should ever again have to live in fear of preaching the Word of God in our country.

Sidney F. Alford, May 2009

Chapter 1
Original Material from Della Tyler Key

DELLA TYLER KEY

This volume is affectionately dedicated to
My Mother,
and to
James (Jim) Reed
Who was an inspiration and a source of much information
about the early days of Texas.

*"Blessed are they that do His commandments,
that they may have right to the
tree of life, and may enter in
through the gates into the city."
Revelation 22nd chapter, 14th verse*

TWO BAPTIST PIONEER PREACHERS OF TEXAS

REED

The name of Reed is believed by some authorities to have been taken from the Scotch word reid, meaning "a reed or hollow stalk." However, others claim that it was taken from the Saxon raed, meaning "speech or discourse" and still others from Rhea, the goddess of ancient Greek mythology. It is found on the ancient English and American records, spelled in various forms. The use of any single spelling of the name does not indicate that all the descendants or ancestors of the individual used the same form.

Families of Reed immigrated to America and settled in New England previous to the middle of the seventeenth century, and the following century, several families immigrated and settled for the most part in Virginia and Maryland.

Descendants of the various branches of the family in America have spread to practically every state in the union. When the first United States census was taken, numerous families of the name were living in Virginia, South Carolina, North Carolina and in other parts of the country.

One of the most ancient of the many Coats-of-Arms of the Reed is described as follows:

Arms—"Or, on a chevron between three garbs gules, as many ears of wheat, stalked and leaved Argent."

NATHANIEL (NATHAN) REED, a Scotchman, was married to an Irish woman, probably about 1770 or 1775. He lived in the Pendleton District of South Carolina, which was at the above date a Cherokee province. However, this territory was taken from the Indians and annexed to

Ninety Six District. In 1791, it was called Washington County. In 1798, Washington County was divided into Greenville and Pendleton Districts, with Pendleton as the county seat of Pendleton District. In 1826 another division was made; Pendleton was divided into Pickens and Anderson Counties and is known by that name today.

Little information is available about Nathan Reed, though he is known to have had two sons, William and Issac.

In the United States census, 1790, of the Ninety-Six District, Pendleton County, South Carolina, Nathional Reed (possibly the above Reed) is reported as the head of a family of five white dependants, and two colored slaves. This list included two white male dependants, with ages under the above sixteen years. Issac, son of Nathan, is known to have been fourteen years old at the time. This would indicate William as the eldest son. Nothing is known of William except that he removed to Tennessee.

ISSAC REED, Baptist preacher and founder of the oldest existing Baptist church in Texas today, son of Nathan Reed and his wife, was born June 6, 1776, in the Pendleton District of South Carolina. Nearby the Cherokee roamed, and wild animals made their homes in the neighboring forests. Issac was born scarcely one month before the Declaration of Independence while troops gathered and alarms spread. His early childhood was lived under the shadow of war. Brave men were shedding their blood for freedom; a nation was being born.

Mr. Reed grew to manhood in South Carolina and in September 1797 he was married to Miss Elizabeth Harper. In 1805 he removed with his family to Franklin County, Tennessee. There at the age of thirty-one, he was ordained a Baptist minister. The following is a copy of the ordination papers:

"The State of Tennessee, Franklin County,
Hopewell Baptist Church;
These are to certify that we being duly called as a presbytery
have examined into the character and call and qualifications of
our beloved brother, Issac Reed, and with the consent of the church
to which he belongs, have by prayer and imposition of hands set him
apart to the work of the ministry and he is hereby authorized to exercise
himself in the several parts of the ministerial function, where he in the
providence of God may be called, whether statedly or occasionally."

Given under our hands this 19th day of March, 1808
John Davis, Abraham Hargis, George Foster, William Jennings

The succeeding twenty-five years Mr. Reed labored with the Baptist Church in western Tennessee. A man of strong personality, earnest and sincere; ever true to his convictions, he became a power for good in the work which he had chosen. He served as moderator of his association and was one of the most outstanding Baptist preachers in the state.

In 1834, two years preceding the Texas Revolution, he removed to East Texas and settled nine miles north of the town of Nacogdoches. However, he established his permanent home some ten or eleven miles west of the present town of Carthage, to the south of Iron's Bayou. He bought 4,428 acres of land from M.A. Romero, in the Romero league survey, lying directly north of Clayton. This purchase was made and recorded in Nacogdoches, Texas, on October 5, 1835. The Romero league at that date was incorporated in Nacogdoches County, later in Shelby County, but today is included in Panola County.

The county of Nacogdoches, very sparsely settled with Americans, was created March 17, 1836, and organized in 1837. It included an area of 962 square miles, with Nacogdoches as county seat. The oldest city in East Texas, Nacogdoches was established in 1779 during the Hasmai Confederacy at one of the old missions, which was set up in 1716 and named for a Texas tribe of that name. This city was headquarters of Mexican authority in East Texas. The Catholic religion was in control and very intolerant of other religious teaching. Laws were in force restraining the establishment of other religious organizations.

For several years following Reed's removal to Nacogdoches, he encountered strong resistance from both the priest and civil authorities—in such manner that he feared for his life and would not preach openly but went about the vicinity preaching and teaching privately. With this handicap, work for the establishment of the church seemed not to have progressed at all.

However, in the summer immediately following the Battle of San Jacinto, perhaps encouraged by the victory of the Texans, Mr. Reed gathered a few colonists in a grove of large oak trees, four miles north of Nacogdoches, and there he preached to them. They continued their meetings in this grove for some time, holding services under the shade of a giant oak, the long branches like wings covering them (the tree originally had a spread of a hundred feet or more). However, during a severe windstorm a few years ago, its trunk was severed about fifteen feet from the ground. The stump is standing today.

The settlers were denied the right to build a meeting house so, eluding the exact construction of the law, on this same spot they built a large house of red oak logs and called it Liberty School House. This was probably the first combined meeting and schoolhouse constructed in Texas by the colonists for the use of those of the Protestant faith. It is not definitely known at what date the schoolhouse was built. Yet it was standing in 1838, and likely was constructed in the fall or winter of 1836, following the opening of services in the summer under the trees.

What must have been the joy and thankfulness of these pioneers as they met in that log house to worship their God, according to the dictates of their own hearts! And there before the people stood Issac Reed, preaching in exuberance of spirit like a shepherd feeding his flock from the table of the Lord. It is said that his sermons sometimes lasted well into two hours.

On Saturday, May 5th, 1838, Mr. Reed, assisted by R.G. Green, organized the first church in East Texas, and they called it "Union" or "Old North Church." Nine members were in the organization; two were colored slaves. Though there is some dispute about this, it is likely the first baptism in Texas was administered that day in May, as B.F. Whitaker was received into the church with that ordinance. Every meeting following saw new additions, some by letter, others by experience and baptism.

The year Union Church was organized, in the winter when the ground was frozen over, Reed's son, Issac Reed (who had married a daughter of Abner Herrin, brother to Lemuel Herrin, Baptist preacher) was killed by the Indians in Panola County. A great revival was conducted in 1839 by Mr. Reed. Many were baptized and received into the church—the first ever baptized in East Texas.

Beloved by his congregation, he continued as pastor of "Old North Church" for nine years following its organization.

Mr. Reed's work was not confined solely to the church of which he was pastor, but he was busy in other parts of the country round about. In 1840, some three miles from the present town of Clayton and ten miles west of Carthage in Panola County (Panola at this time was incorporated in Nacogdoches County), with the assistance of Mr. Lemuel Herrin (Baptist preacher who had moved to Texas in 1841), Issac Reed organized in his own house the Bethel church. Later, when Clayton was built, the

"OLD NORTH CHURCH"

In 1863, some years after Issac Reed's death, the old log building was moved a little distance away, and the building above erected on the spot where the first one stood. This has been in use as a church for eighty-five years, and today has a membership of about twenty. In the foreground is the stump of the old tree under which services were first held.

church was moved into town. On the spot where the church was first organized, today there stands a Negro church. Many trees are growing in the vicinity, and the church is located in a grove of oak trees. Every year the Negroes celebrate the anniversary of their freedom there. They come for miles around, the evening before, and spend the night at the church. The next day they enjoy singing and preaching and a big barbecue. In the afternoon, baseball is usually played.

In 1843, Mr. Reed, together with Lemuel Herrin, constituted Border Church in Harrison County. The presbyter was composed of the above, with eight members.

In Harrison County, west of Carthage, on Saturday before the first Sunday in April, 1845, these two men constituted Macedonia church, with a membership of sixteen.

The need was felt for a general association, and in 1843 representatives from five churches met in the "Old North Church." There with Issac Reed, Lemuel Herrin, and Asa Wright presiding, they organized the Sabine Association. In 1846 they had a membership of three hundred with Mr. Reed as moderator. In 1847, the membership was five hundred twenty seven, with William Britton as moderator. But soon the association became divided and in the end was dissolved, because of internal doctrinal dissensions.

Much of the blame was laid upon the shoulders of Mr. Reed, because of the missionary views which he held. Writers have been unable to understand his attitude, and certain members of the association could not. Lemuel Herrin, as a missionary in favor of boards and societies, opposed him very sharply. He was accused of retarding progress of the church, of seeking popularity and of revolting against the very cause which he had claimed with so much zeal. But surely, it was not popularity which he sought; neither denied he the cause for which he stood. He believed in missionary work, but objected to boards and missionary societies, and the church in East Texas, for a time, followed his teaching. But after a time, the latter element gaining power opposed his views on this matter. Doubtless, at his age (three score and ten), he found it hard to summon the tact with which to meet the situation. He died in 1848. It was sometime after his death that the association was dissolved.

Issac Reed was, without doubt, vastly superior to the average preacher. A positive character, successful in winning many souls to Christ, he died February 1848 and was buried in the "Old Bethel Church" graveyard in Panola County. His grave is marked by a rude stone.

In the city of Nacogdoches, February 1848, his Will was probated and filed, signed with his mark, as he was doubtless too ill to write at the time the Will was made. He owned in Panola County about 7,000 acres of land and a number of slaves, which he equally divided among his children at his death.

Mr. Reed was a medium large man with black hair. He married in September 1797 to Miss Elizabeth Harper, born March 20, 1779. From this union were born four boys and four girls: Issac H; William, born in South Carolina July 12, 1798; John, Baptist preacher, who remained in Tennessee; Samuel; and daughters Mary, Elizabeth, Margaret, and Frankie.

WILLIAM B. REED, first Judge of Hamilton County, Texas, was born July 12, 1798, in South Carolina. He was the son of Issac Reed, Baptist preacher.

In 1808, William removed with his father to Franklin County, Tennessee. There he married in 1817 Miss Sarah Wright.

In 1834, he again removed with his father to East Texas, and secured several thousand acres of land in that part which is now Rusk County. He made his home on his farm about three miles northeast of Mount Enterprise.

Rusk County, the upper East Texas timbered region, created and organized in 1843 from Nacogdoches County, was named for Thomas Rusk, who was born in Pendleton District, South Carolina in 1803. In this county, nearly a century after William Reed had settled there, oil was discovered, which proved to be from the richest pool in the world.

The colonization act had been passed in Texas in 1825 as an inducement to settlement, which promised to every head of a family (if a farmer) 177 acres of farming land and 4,428 acres of pasture for stock, to be exempt from taxes for six years after date of settlement. There was an abundance of wild game, fruits and nuts, and the climate was mild. However, for one to obtain land in Texas, allegiance must be sworn to the Catholic Church, or purchase made.

Records are not available to show how William Reed acquired his land in East Texas, although it is to be hoped (and probably so) that he followed the example of his father and kept faith with the church.

Mr. Reed farmed and raised cattle, sheep and hogs. He owned a number of slaves. A man of some education, he taught school when he was a young man, and used to doctor among his friends and neighbors, principally with the plant Lobelia, which was remarkable as an emetic. A deacon in the Baptist Church, he took a prominent part in church affairs.

After living twenty-four years in Rusk County, Mr. Reed sold his land and on March 1, 1860, together with other members of the family, set out west for a new location. They took their livestock and a number of slaves, and traveled in wagons drawn by oxen.

On the 4th day of September, they landed in Hamilton County on Honey Creek, three miles east of where Carlton now stands.

The settlement at Honey Creek, which consisted of but four families, welcomed the weary travelers warmly.

The country round about was beautiful with green trees, wild flowers,

Issac Reed, grandson of Issac Reed

grass and streams of water. Fish were plentiful, and droves of deer, antelope, wild turkey and prairie chicken were there in abundance.

On account of Indian raids (which were frequent in those days) and because they were able to secure land there, the Reeds all settled near each other on Honey Creek.

William Reed took an active part in the affairs of the community. Very accurate in business matters, his word was considered as good as gold. He was elected first judge of Hamilton County. It is said that the first court was held under a large oak tree, located where the courthouse now stands. He was serving in this capacity at his death from smallpox in 1863, when a severe epidemic of this disease swept through the community. Many died; all were prostrated, so that there was scarcely left those able to bury the dead. Mr. Reed's family were all ill and a son, Pleasant, who was married and living on Honey Creek, died and was the first one buried in Honey Creek Cemetery, which was set up on land owned by the Reeds. William Reed was the next to be entered there.

William H. Reed, born July 12, 1798 in South Carolina, died March 1, 1863.

Married in 1817 in Tennessee.

Miss Sarah Wright, born July 2, 1800 died and was buried in Honey Creek beside her husband.

Eleven children were born to this union: Pleasant, born May 14, 1818; Elizabeth, Mary, Issac, John, James (Jim), Margaret, Lydia, Bridget, Catherine, and Amanda.

ISSAC REED, Baptist preacher, born February 1, 1825. The son of William Reed, Baptist deacon and grandson of Issac Reed, Baptist preacher.

At the age of nine years, young Reed accompanied his father and grandfather to East Texas. Before leaving Tennessee he had been converted to the faith and baptized by Lemuel Herrin, Baptist preacher. He grew to manhood in Rusk County and at an early age married Miss Elizabeth Tolbert.

When the church in East Texas became torn with dissension because of missionary doctrine, missionaries were excluded from the church. Issac Reed and a number of his family members were among those excluded.

In 1860 Reed, with his father and other members of the family, removed to Hamilton County where he made his home seven miles west of Hico on Honey Creek. At that time, Hico was a small village of not more than three families. Soon after this, L.D. Stringer, Baptist preacher, went to the home of Issac Reed for the purpose of securing his services to preach for the church in Hico. Mr. Reed had been licensed to preach in East Texas, but had not been ordained, possibly because of the dissension in the church there. So, turning very pale, perhaps under deep emotion, he said to Mr. Stringer, "I am only licensed to preach." However Mr. Stringer insisted that he take up the work there, which he consented to do.

After preaching a few times at the church in Hico, in 1861 the Reeds went into the constitution of Mount Zion church there, under the direction of A.D. Maroney and L.D. Stringer. Upon this same occasion Mr. Reed was ordained as minister and called to the care of Mount Zion Church as their first pastor. This was the beginning of his work for the church in his new home.

He served the church at Hico for some time during which the church was a member of the Leon River Association.

Mr. Reed seems to have left this church during the Civil War and removed to Erath County. He lived at Dublin for some time and was pastor of the church there which was then a member of the Brazos River Association and known as Leon, but in 1872 it was reorganized as Dublin. It is not known for how long he was pastor of the Leon Church, although his first wife, Elizabeth, died and was buried in the "Old Dublin Cemetery" in 1864. He was probably serving the Dublin church at this time.

The Reeds were in the organization of Honey Creek Church in Hamilton County, 1867. However, in 1871, D.D. Mullins was pastor of this church. Honey Creek church today is the oldest existing Baptist church in Hamilton County.

Mr. Reed constituted Macedonia Church in Erath County August 7, 1871, with fourteen members.

In the Session of the Brazos River Association held with Round Grove Church, September 1872, Issac Reed was to have preached the introductory sermon, as the minutes state that "in the absence of Issac Reed the introductory sermon was preached by Elder Northcutt."

Honey Creek Church at Hico was believed to have been constituted by Mr. Reed. He was pastor there from August 1873 to June 1876 and also listed in the minutes of the Session of the Bosque River Association, held in August 1874 with Honey Creek Church, Erath County, as pastor of Honey Creek Church. During the time he was pastor there, the session of the Brazos River Association for the year 1875 was held at Honey Creek Church. The minutes of the Bosque River Association, held in Pleasant Grove Baptist Church, Bosque County, August 1876, lists Issac Reed as ordained minister at Meridian, Bosque County.

The Minutes of this Association held at Mount Zion Church, Hico, Texas, August 1879, lists Mr. Reed as messenger and clerk from Meridian Creek Church. His post office address, Cranfill Gap.

In the proceedings of the Association, the chairman of the committee for reporting on temperance submitted the following report:

"We, your committee on temperance, submit the following report. That we in our judgment think the subject of temperance has been exhausted on paper; we would

therefore recommend to this body and the churches composing it: the strict observance of the Bible, and put the evil from among us."

Issac Reed
H. Holey
A.V. Neely

In Erath County October 1879, Issac Reed together with Mr. J.F. Cook constituted Oak Grove No. 2, with thirteen members. This church still exists but is independent and does not cooperate with any association or convention.

Mr. Reed and J.R. Northcutt constituted Live Oak Church in Erath County in May, 1880, with ten members. The church is today a member of the Erath County Baptist Association. Reed was a member of this church at the time of his death in 1908.

"The first Annual Session of the Honey Grove Baptist Association, held with Honey Grove Church, Fannin County, July 1880. (Issac Reed is listed in the Minutes as messenger from Bells Church, Grayson County, though Bragg is pastor.)

Brethren Issac Reed, J.L. May, W.M. Carter, E.M. Hunt, and W.A. Benedict were to "prepare a Constitution, Articles of Faith, and rules of order."

"On Foreign Missions," Issac Reed, F. Jones and A.J. Crittendon—and Mr. Reed was to preach the evening sermon. They sang the song "Oh, For A Closer Walk with God."

The Association reassembled at 2 p.m. and prayer was said by Mr. Reed. He was appointed with others to compose a home mission board. H.F. Jones was recommended and adopted as their beneficiary, to which Issac Reed pledged five dollars. He was among those appointed by the moderator as chairman of the standing committee on "Home Mission Board."

The following resolution was proposed:

"Resolved that for convenience in our general mission work, we cooperate with North Texas Baptist Missionary Convention." Signed by Brethren E.M. Hunt, Issac Reed, and others.

Appendix B. Foreign Mission:

"The foreign mission work is no longer an experiment. Its success has been beyond expectation. The Savior's injunction, 'Preach the Gospel to every creature,' still remains. In the past few years, the work in foreign fields has been more richly blessed than at home. In the last two years, nearly thirty thousand have been baptized in Burma alone. We have mission stations now in China, Africa, Italy, Brazil, and Mexico. The largest Baptist church in the world is where the name of Christ was not known a few years ago, and was built up under missionary labor. Men who feel it their duty to preach in foreign lands are now waiting; but our board is unable to support them. As Christ has redeemed us and given us the joys of salvation, we should be ready to extend it to others. As the Lord has prospered us, let us aid in this great work of bringing to the world the knowledge of Christ."

Signed: Issac Reed, Chairman

In the 'Sixth Annual Session of the Comanche Baptist Association held with Mount Pleasant Baptist Church, Erath County,' September 1880: Oak Grove and Live Oak Churches were admitted into the Association.

A 'Committee on Books and Periodicals' was appointed and composed of Issac Reed, William Northcutt, and S.E. Bullard.

At 2 O'clock P.M. the Association was called to order and prayer by Issac Reed.

Monday morning, 'the report on Books and Periodicals' was as follows:

"We recommend the Bible as the first and last book, the book of all books and the only guide of our faith and practice. Study it, brethren, by the aid of the Holy Spirit and follow its teachings. Also that there are many good religious books and periodicals that are sound in doctrine, profitable for instruction, but we would leave each of these to commend itself on its own merits."

Signed: Issac Reed, Chairman

"The Session of the Honey Grove Baptist Association held with Little Jordan Church, Fannin County, August 1881.

The clerk being absent, Issac Reed was appointed clerk, pro tem. The Association then elected Elder B.I. Smith as moderator and Mr. Reed as clerk permanent.

On motion the meeting adjourned until 3 O'clock to hear a sermon on 'The Difference between Baptists and all other Denominations, on the Plan of Salvation,' by Issac Reed, who took his text from Ephesians 2:8, 9: 8. *For by grace are ye saved through faith; and that not of yourselves; it is the gift of God;* 9. *Not of works, lest any man should boast.*

The meeting was reassembled and "on motion of Issac Reed, agreed that any member of this body be a corresponding messenger in any of the Associations around us on presenting a Minute of this Association with his own name on it."

On motion of J.L. May, the Association requested Mr. Reed to superintend the printing and distribution of the minutes and to receive five dollars for the same.

El. B.F. Smith, moderator of the Association and Mr. Reed elected clerk. Reed is also named as messenger and pastor from Bell's Church.

In the "Session of this Association held with White Mound Church, Grayson County," August 1882, Mr. B.I. Smith was moderator and Reed is again elected clerk, and is asked to superintend the printing and distribution of the minutes and to receive ten dollars for his services.

Mr. Reed is named as pastor and messenger again from Bells Church; post-office, Bells.

"The Session of the Association held with the Bells Church, Grayson County, August 1883, Mr. J.L. May was moderator and Mr. A.T. Wilcon clerk. Issac Reed is again listed as pastor and messenger from Bells Church.

Mr. Reed was on the committee "On Sunday Schools."

A prayer was said by Mr. J.B. Link.

Upon the 'Report on Temperance', "that we advise the churches to withdraw fellowship from every brother who is a habitual dram drinker;" addresses were made by Mr. Reed and others upon the report.

The report upon the state of the churches was read. Speeches were made by Reed and J.L. Mays. The report was adopted.

Appendix D:

"The committee on Sunday Schools would suggest there seems to be a growing interest in Sunday Schools in the Association and we would urge greater activity and teaching the same doctrine to children that we do to parents. We would recommend the appointment of a Sunday School Evangelist in this Association in cooperation with the State Board."

Signed: Issac Reed, Chairman

In the Session of the Association held with Owen Chapel Church, Fannin County, August 1884, Mr. J.L. Mays is named as pastor of Bells Church. No mention is made of Mr. Reed in the minutes of the Association in the Sessions of 1885 and 1886.

The minutes of the "Comanche Baptist Association 16th Annual Session held with Desdemona Church, Eastland County, September 1890" reports on Issac Reed, as ordained minister at Dublin but does not list him as pastor of any church. In the minutes of this Association in 1891, 1892, 1893, 1895, 1897 he is listed the same as the above.

A great deal could be written about the primitive ways of living, of their methods of farming and the discouraging privations endured by the settlers in the early days, in this part of the state. Coal was made from large pine logs which were placed in a large ditch and covered over with dirt and leaves. A small opening was left in which to set fire to the logs; when this was done, all openings were closed and the logs usually took four or five days to burn out. The charcoal was used as coal. Grease for greasing wagons and other implements of that nature was made from burning pine logs, also. The rich logs were placed upon ground which had previously been burned until it was hard; fire was set and the tar which ran from the logs was caught in a bucket placed in a trench nearby.

The settlers were forced to be always on the lookout for the red man. The Comanche Indians were a constant menace, killing and stealing and destroying the property of the settlers. This continued for many years after the Civil War. Issac Reed rode a horse round about the country to do his preaching and he was never without the protection of his six-shooter. Often during church services his gun and Bible were laid side by side.

The settlers went to church in their wagons or many of the younger ones perhaps rode horses. Services were held under brush arbors and many of their homes were built of logs or rough lumber.

The names of all the churches which Mr. Reed pastored are not known; however, most of his preaching was done in Bosque, Coryell, and Hamilton counties.

Reed was usually referred to as "The Old Irishman." Though an uneducated man, he was possessed of a strong countenance and a good delivery. His sermons were prolonged but not tedious. Irish and witty, often during a sermon he diverted his audience by relating an amusing incident, though he used it as an illustration to impress some vital truth. He was said to have been, in his day, by far the best preacher of any other in that section of the country. One brother preacher remarked of him, that "Issac Reed was the deepest man he had ever conversed with, not to be an educated man." He loved to talk, not upon things immaterial but upon things of worth. An interesting talker, he engaged the attention of any gathering in public or at one's own fireside.

Musical instruments were not tolerated in the church until long after the Civil War. Foot washing was practiced as an ordinance till some time in the eighties. Every member of the church was expected to attend all services. If one were absent two Sundays in succession, a good reason must be given.

Standing during prayer was not permitted; all were expected to kneel.

In the singing, ordinarily the preacher read the entire hymn through; then, after again reading the first two lines, these were sung and after that the next two lines were read and sung. This procedure continued on through to the end of the song. The names of a number of the favorite songs were: *Amazing Grace, How Firm A Foundation, Holy Manna, Show Pity, Lord, Children of the Heavenly King,* and others. The old hymn books contained hundreds of songs; a few of these are included in our books today.

When Issac Reed conducted a service, he usually led the singing. One of his favorite hymns was *"Oh, How I Love Jesus."* He had a good voice and loved to sing. People loved to hear him sing. When James Reed, who was a child of five at the time, heard his "Uncle Ike" coming up the road singing, he stopped his play and begged the other children to listen to the song, which he recalled contained these words: "When the warfare is over, hallelujah!"

During the Civil War, Mr. Reed conducted a meeting near Hico on the banks of the Bosque. At its close, on a Sunday noon, there were several candidates for the ordinance of baptism. The crowd went about three-quarters of a mile up the river to a place which was ideal for baptizing. The bank was covered in gravel and shaded by trees. The water was clear, and about six or eight feet from the bank, it was deep enough for that purpose.

Mr. Daniel Shipman was present and had been requested to baptize his nephew, who was a candidate for the ordinance. Mr. Shipman went about the matter very energetically. He grabbed the young man by the arm, rushed him into the water and quickly administered the act of baptism. He remarked as he came out of the water, "I just believe that is the way Christ went into the water." Cam Self, a young man sitting on the banks of the river, with a big laugh said, "Parson, do you think that he went in as fast as you did?"

James Reed, who was a small lad at this time, was sitting with another boy on a log across the river watching the procedure. He relates that "Issac Reed then went on with baptizing the other candidates, and that among the spectators was 'Old Man Abe Lee' and wife. On such occasions it was customary for Mrs. Lee, overcome by religious fervor, to throw up her arms and shout. Anticipating this, Mr. Lee took their baby in his arms. But soon however, overpowered by the scene, he himself was shouting 'Hallelujah.' He threw the child up in his arms, and it would have fallen to the ground, had it not been for Amanda Reed and other women standing close by, who caught it as it fell."

Mr. Reed used the following in a sermon, preached at Old Rock Church, Hamilton County: "A certain woman, discovering a cow in the field, cried out, 'A cow is in the field, a cow is in the field!' A man with answer sure and simple, said, 'Put the cow out and close the gate.'" This was possibly used to illustrate the truth that one should not merely cry out against sin, but that it should be driven out and the entrance closed.

Mrs. J.A. Barnes, a granddaughter of Issac Reed, remembers hearing him preach on the resurrection. He took his text from First John. Upon another occasion, in services held at Pecan School House, Hamilton

County, he preached about the 'unpardonable sin.'

While living on Honey Creek, he owned a blacksmith shop in which he worked. It was located across the street from the home of his brother, Pleasant. One day as he started for work, his niece came running to tell him that Bill Herrin (brother to Amanda Reed, wife of Pleasant), whom Reed had known and loved since childhood, had come for a visit. Turning about, he went immediately to see his old friend and they stood there, hands clasped, looking into each other's faces, with deep love and respect written therein.

After some conversation, a question about the Scriptures was introduced. This resulted in a prolonged discussion of things pertaining to the Bible, in which they were engaged until the evening meal. Afterward the chairs were removed to the yard (as it was summertime) and the two sat there in earnest conversation until the chickens were crowing for day.

Such was the life of a man who gave himself to the church; always interested in his Master's word and work.

The last years of his life were spent quietly in Dublin, where he lived in his home there with his second wife, Rebecca, who survived him by a year. He died June 25, 1908, and was buried in Old Dublin Cemetery, which is located about two and one-half miles southeast of Dublin.

This inscription is carved upon his tombstone:

"IN THEE, O LORD, HAVE I PUT MY TRUST."

Issac Reed had red hair, which bushed up, and he wore a beard which never grew very long. He was of medium height and weighed about one hundred seventy-five pounds.

He was married first to Miss Elizabeth Tolbert, born December 6th, 1826, and died April 22, 1864. By Elizabeth he had seven children. He married second Mrs. Rebecca Cranfill Smith, born March 6th, 1834 and died July 11, 1909. By Rebecca he had four children. Both wives are buried in Old Dublin Cemetery. Mr. Reed lies between them.

Chapter 2
Reed Genealogy compiled by Della Tyler Key

The Reed Genealogy

NATHAN OR NATHANIEL REED, Scotchman. Married an Irish woman. Children:
1. William, removed to Tennessee and became the owner of land there.
2. Issac, born June 6, 1776, Pendleton District, South Carolina, died Feb. 1848, Panola County, Texas

ISSAC REED, born June 6, 1776. Married in 1797 in South Carolina to Miss Elizabeth Harper, born March 20, 1779. Children:
1. William B., born July 12, 1798
2. John H., Baptist preacher, remained in Tennessee
3. Issac M.A. Herrin, killed by Indians 1838 in Panola County
4. Samuel
5. Mary, married Henry Aswalt
6. Elizabeth, married Hugh Sheppard
7. Margaret, married William Roark
8. Frankie, married John Morris

WILLIAM B. REED, born July 12, 1798, died March 1, 1863, buried in Honey Creek Cemetery. Married Sarah Wright, born July 2, 1880. Children:
1. Pleasant, born July 2, 1818; died Feb. 14, 1863. Married Amanda Melvina Herrin
2. Elizabeth, married Issac Morris
3. Mary, married Joseph Ferguson
4. Issac, married Elizabeth Tolbert
5. John, married Emaline Herrin

6. Jim, married Nancy Ward
7. Margaret, married Herman Ward
8. Lydia, married Richard Feglee
9. Bridget, married Greenville Norris, 2nd Joe Phillips
10. Catherine, married George Bushing
11. Amanda, youngest, born Jan. 1831, died Feb. 8, 1800, buried in Dublin. Married R.M. O'Neal; 2nd, William Goodson.

Children of William B. Reed and Sarah Wright Reed

PLEASANT REED, born July 12, 1798, died March 1, 1863. Married in Rusk County Amanda Melvina Herrin (died March 3, 1884), daughter Lemuel Herrin, Baptist preacher. Children all born in Rusk County.
1. William (Bill H.) born Nov. 6, 1844, died Dec. 13, 1929. Served in Civil War. Married 1st Sarah Rosilee Blackstock, married 2nd Mrs. Kate Jones.
2. Lemuel D., born July 17, 1846 (Ranger service)
3. Mary (Pollie) born April 22, 1848, married T.F. Montgomery
4. James (Jim) born April 2, 1850, married Nancy Eveline Richard
5. Emily, born April 5, 1852, married Wheeler Lee.
6. Elizabeth, born July 30, 1854, died Sept. 27, 1851
7. Sarah, born Feb. 21, 1856, died
8. Issac, born June 6, 1872, died July 26, 1872 Hamilton County
9. Richard, born Jan. 12, 1861 in Hamilton County

ISSAC REED, born Feb. 1, 1825, died June 25, 1908. Married first at an early age Miss Elizabeth Tolbert. Children:
1. Nancy Jane, born 1846, married John L. Berkley
2. Elizabeth, married Arch Blancett
3. John (Baptist preacher), married _____ Casper.
4. William (Bill), married widow Smith who had one son, Alf Smith

5. Pleas, married _____
6. Martha, died in infancy

Reed married 2nd Rebecca Cranfill Smith (a lovely woman with three daughters, Kate, Ella, and Mollie). Children:
1. Bird, died in infancy
2. Erasmus (Ross), only one of family left living in 1938
3. Tom, youngest, married widow Long. Killed in car wreck.

Children of Pleasant Reed and Amanda Melvina Herrin Reed:
1. William (Bill) Reed, born Nov. 6, 1844; died Dec. 13, 1929. Married Jan. 6, 1876 in Hamilton County to Sarah Rosilee Blackstock, born Sept. 18, 1856, died Feb. 10, 1900. Five children by this marriage. William married 2nd 1905 Mrs. Kate Jones. There were no children. William served in Civil War for its duration. He is buried in Honey Creek Cemetery beside his first wife and about twenty feet from his grandfather's grave.
2. Lemuel D. Reed, born July 17, 1846 (saw Ranger service and took part in an Indian fight), died Nov. 14, 1934 at Littlefield (Lamb County). Married Sept. 27, 1877 Hanna Montgomery (died Feb. 1935). Ten children.
3. Mary (Pollie) Reed, born Apr. 22, 1848, Married April 20, 1871, J.F. Montgomery, died Sept. 25, 1933.
4. James (Jim) Reed, born April 2, 1850, died Mar. 10, 1939. Buried in Dublin. Married March 15, 1876 Nancy Eveline Richards, died Jan. 17, 1934. Nine children.
5. Emily Reed, born Apr. 5, 1856, died some years ago in Haskell County, Married March 16, 1876 in Hamilton County. Married Wheeler Lee who died some years ago in Haskell County. Six children.
6. Elizabeth Reed, born July 30, 1854, died Sept. 27, 1859.
7. Sarah Reed, born Feb. 21, 1856, died in infancy.

8. Issac Reed, born June 6, 1872, died July 26, 1872 in Hamilton County.
9. Richard Reed, born Jan. 12, 1861 in Hamilton County, died at Meadow, Terry County. Married. Two children.

NANCY JANE REED, born 1846, died Oct. 18, 1928. Married about 1869 at Desdemona John Linton Berkley, born Apr. 19, 1825, died Aug. 2, 1896. Children:
1. Infant, died
2. Magnolia, born June 1, 1871, married Jim Cole
3. Thomas Issac, born Feb. 1, 1873, bachelor
4. May Belle, born May 23, 1879, married 1st R.D. Tyler, 2nd Amos Guinn
5. Robert E. Lee, born Feb. 28, 1876, died Feb. 2, 1892
6. Hubert and Jepthy L., born June 23, 1884. Hubert married Ownie; Jepthy married Fannie
7. Boy born Oct. 16, 1886, died 1886
8. Minnie Lee, born Oct. 16, 1886, died Dec. 24, 1917, married Ead Hughes, died 1917. Both buried in Goodwell, Oklahoma

ELIZABETH REED, born possibly 1859. Married 1874 in Hamilton, Texas, Arch D. Blancett, born about 1864. Both died and buried at Hamilton. Children:
1. Charlie, married Susie Partridge
2. Ellen, married 1st Strawn Morgan, married 2nd Jim A. Barnes
3. Dee, married Myrtle Partridge
4. Leaner, married W.L. Richardson
5. John, died at two and a half years
6. Clem, married Louise Key
7. Roy, married Billie Munix

All the above children were living in and around Hamilton in 1938.

Children of Nancy Reed Berkley and John Linton Berkley

MAGNOLIA BERKLEY, born June 1, 1871. Married in Hamilton County Jim Cole. Eight Children: Jessie, Maude, Myrtle, Authur, Bolding, Mary, May Belle, Robert

MAY BELLE BERKLEY, born May 23, 1879. Married Aug. 30, 1896 Hamilton County Radolph D. Tyler, born Nov. 5, 1870, died Dec. 22, 1935. Children:
1. Claude Lee, married Jessie Kate Housden
2. Della, married Laurence M. Key
3. Ayra May, married Lon Byars.

Children of MayBelle Berkley Tyler and Radolph Tyler

CLAUDE LEE, born July 6, 1897, in Hamilton County. Married March 1933, Miss Jessie Kate Housden. Children:
1. Irvin, adopted, born Dec. 9, 1926
2. Bobbie, born Sept. 15, 1934
3. Joyce Ann, born Dec. 20, 1935
4. Claude Jr., born 1938

DELLA TYLER, born Dec. 8, 1898 in Hamilton County. Married Jan. 22, 1916, at Vernon, Texas, to Laurence Macager Key, born July 1, 1894. Children:
1. Laurence Macager Key, Jr., born Sept. 14, 1918, Vernon, Texas
2. Geraldine Corrin Key, born Aug. 27, 1923, Amarillo, Texas, died August 1923

AYRA MAY TYLER, born March 2, 1900, in Hamilton County. Married Jan. 22, 1916, Vernon, Texas to Lon Byars, Jr. born 1896, died Aug. 3, 1927, buried at Vernon. Children:
1. Gordon Byars, born Sept. 2, 1918

L.M. KEY, Jr. born Sept. 14, 1918, married Dec. 7, 1937 at Pampa, Texas to Evelyn Carroll.

GORDON BYARS, born Sept. 2, 1918. Married Dec. 15, 1937, at Amarillo, Texas, to Martha Lee King. Died Aug. 25, 1961.

Chapter 3
Reference Information from Key's Book

REFERENCE IS MADE TO THE FOLLOWING:
- The Dublin Progress—1938
- Dallas Morning News—1938
- Mr. A.S. Salley, Secretary Historical Commission, South Carolina
- The Media Research Bureau, Washington, D.C.
- Mr. James Reed, Dublin, Texas
- Dr. D.D. Tidwell
- Centennial Story of Texas, Baptist pub., 1936
- Flowers and Fruits by Z.N. Morrell (1872)
- History of the Baptists of Texas by B.F. Riley (1900)
- History of Texas Baptists by J.M. Carroll (1923)
- Baptist Standard, Mar. 25, 1920, page 22
- Texas Historical and Biographical Magazine, Vol. 1, 1892 by J.B. Link
- With the Makers of Texas by Bolton and Barker
- The minutes of the Brazos River Association, 1872
- The minutes of the Bosque River Association, 1876-1879
- The minutes of the Honey Grove Association, 1880
- The minutes of the Comanche Baptist Association, 1880, 1882, 1883, 1884
- The Texas Almanac and State Industrial Guide—1936
- History and Biography of Texas by Z.T. Fulmore as told in county name

Chapter 4
Additional Information

An additional piece of family information came from the writings of Ralph T. Reed:[2]

Rev. Issac Reed Family

Issac Reed was born June 6, 1776, in Pendleton, Anderson County, South Carolina. He was the son of Nathaniel Reed (born 1749) and Hepsibah Bateman Reed. He married Elizabeth Harper in South Carolina in 1797. They moved to Franklin County, Tennessee in 1805 where Issac was ordained a Baptist minister in 1808.

Prior to 1835 the family moved to Nacogdoches, Texas. Several of their married children and families came with Rev. Issac. In October 1835 Rev. Issac bought from Citizen Manuel Antonio Romero a league and labor of land located in what is now Panola County. He also acquired land in Rusk County near the present site of Mt. Enterprise. At least four of the families moved to an area some three miles northwest of Clayton, built homes, and cleared land along a spring branch on a road or trail from Shreveport to Nacogdoches via Grand Bluff Ferry across the Sabine River. They also built a fort for protection, which proved wise according to the History of Fairplay by S.T. Allison in which he says, "That fall the Indians became hostile and Elijah Allred went to Rev. Issac Reed's. While he was there, Issac Reed, Jr. was killed by an Indian. By piecing bits of history together, this was in February 1837. It happened this way:

The Whites had been forted up for several days. Not seeing any sign of Indians for a few days, it was decided late one afternoon to investigate what the Indians had done. On arriving at the home of Hugh Sheppard, a light was seen in his corncrib. It proved to be Indians. An Indian shot Issac Reed, Jr. When Reed fell, the others, thinking him to be dead, ran to the fort. After arriving, they could hear Reed calling, but as it was getting dark, they all hesitated to go. One old Negro said he would go even if he got killed; so he carried Reed to the fort. Reed told of raising up on his elbow, taking aim, and shooting at an Indian, but didn't know whether he hit him or not. Reed died during the night. The Indian was found dead next morning, thrown in the branch with brush over him. Issac Reed, Jr. and Elijah Allred married sisters, daughters of Abner Herrin.

Rev. Issac Reed had a daughter, a Mrs. Roark, who lived near the present site of Mt. Enterprise, a distance of about 25 miles. It was decided to send Allred to tell them. Allred said it was a bright moonlit night, the ground was frozen, and he thought he had never heard a horse make so much noise. There was not any lumber with which to make a coffin; so young Reed was wrapped in a blanket and buried in Old Bethel Cemetery, the first white man buried in this section."

In Old Bethel Cemetery are four grave markers of native stone. Two are chiseled and polished to resemble head and shoulders of a human. They have no names or dates. In 1936 the State of Texas erected granite memorial markers in the cemetery and at Church Bethel in Clayton.

In 1838 Rev. Issac organized Old North Church near Nacogdoches, which is the oldest Baptist Church in Texas. In his home Rev. Issac, assisted by Rev. Lemuel Herrin, a minister from the same area of Tennessee, organized Bethel Baptist Church. Old Bethel is on the original site and is now an active Negro Church. Church Bethel was moved to Clayton in the 1870's and possesses the original minutes of organization of 1843.

Reed's settlement secured a Post Office June 13, 1848 with William Walton as the first Postmaster. It was discontinued Feb. 17, 1868.

By Ralph T. Reed

---

1. Taken from the Texas Almanac online, 2008–2009 version, History of Religion section: http://www.texasalmanac.com/history/highlights/religion/
2. Taken from A History of Panola County, Texas, 1819–1978, published by Panola County Historical Commission, Carthage, Texas; Part I, Written by Leila B. LaGrone

Chapter 5
Photos

Site of the Old North Church north of Nacogdoches. To the left of the marker is the remains of the Oak Tree where Issac Reed first preached.

Old North Church Site

Site of Old North Church First known as Union Church as several denominations joined here to worship as early as 1836. Organized in 1838. A small log church was completed that year on ten acres donated by Dr. John M. Sparks. The present structure dates from 1852. In its graveyard rest many of the leading Anglo-American settlers of Nacogdoches County.

"Under This Tree"
The first Baptist Prayer Meeting was organized in 1835 by Aunt Massy Sparks Millard. Issac Reed in 1835 preached the first Baptist sermon. Issac Reed and Elder R.G. Green organized the first Baptist Church in the State of Texas, the first Sunday in May, 1838, the church known today as "Old North Church." The first Protestant School in Texas was taught in a one-room log house in the shadows of the old oak tree.
"Remember, God alone can make a tree."

Sign at present site of Old North Baptist Church

The picture above is of the North Church (now located on the site of the original Old North Church north of Nacogdoches). In the foreground is the old oak tree stump where Issac Reed first preached sermons in Texas under the shade of the tree.

North Church

Front of North Church today

Side view of North Church today

Old Bethel Cemetery

Rev. Isaac Reed
Pioneer Baptist Minister ~ Born in Tennessee. Came to Texas in 1834. Rev. Reed erected the Old North Church near Nacogdoches in 1838. In 1843 he erected Old Bethel Church. Killed by Indians in 1848. (Marker erected by the State of Texas, 1936)

The above marker at the Old Bethel Cemetery is inaccurate. Issac Reed was born in South Carolina and was not killed by Indians; it was his son who was killed by Indians.

Family Plot in Old Bethel Cemetery

Graves of Issac Reed, his wife Rebecca, and son Issac (who was killed by Indians in 1838). It is believed that the two graves to the right of the marker were Issac and Rebecca and the one on the left was their son, Issac.

Another view of the family plot

Issac Reed's grave markers, hand chiseled, reside in the Old Bethel Cemetery.

The Church that currently sits on the site of the Old Bethel Church is now a black congregation.

Sign at the current Bethel Baptist Church

New Bethel Church Site
Clayton, Texas

Church Bethel
Organized on Saturday before the 4th Lord's Day in September, 1843 by Rev. Issac Reed
A pioneer Baptist minister in his home two miles northwest moved to this spot in 1874.
The original minutes of organization are in the possession of this church.
(Monument erected by the State of Texas 1936)

Bethel Church that sits in Clayton, Texas

Copy of Original Minutes of Bethel Church

At Elder Issac Reed's dwelling house, we the members of the United Baptist order, being met together in the fear of God for the purpose of constituting the Church Bethel, and called on Elders Issac Reed and Abner Herrin to act as Presbytery and Lemull Herrin as clerk protem, the Church covenant being read and approved, Articles of faith being read and approved and we whose names are undersigned were pronounced by the Presbytery the Church Bethel. We then opened the door for the reception of members. Received by letter: Elder Issac Reed, Elder Lemull Herrin into our fellowship, then concluded by prayer. List of names constitute members:

Henry Awalt	Amanda Reed	Elizabeth Barbie
John Morris	Sarah Alred	John Barksdail
Issac Morris	Mary Herrin	Elizabeth Reed
Edwin Sweit	Elder Issac Reed	William Herin
George Sweit	Elder Lemull Herrin	Karon H. Herrin
Abner Herrin	John R. Hartsfield	Percill Reed
Kegia Herrin	Charles C. Scruggs	Francis Morris
Julie Barbie	Elizabeth Scruggs	

Old Dublin Memorial Park

Grandson Issac Reed
is buried in the Dublin cemetery,
with his two wives buried beside him,
one on each side.

INDEX OF MAIN EVENTS

13	Issac Reed, ordained as Baptist minister, 19th day of March 1808
13	Issac Reed moved to East Texas, 1834 (Laws were in force restraining the establishment of religious organizations other than Roman Catholic)
14	Catholic religion was in control in Texas
15	First Baptist church organized in state of Texas
15	Issac Reed, Jr., killed by Indians, 1837
15	Bethel church organized
17	Reed objected to Boards and Missionary Societies
18	Reed buried in Old Bethel Church graveyard, 1848
22	Grandson Issac Reed ordained as minister, 1861
23, 27	Report on Temperance
24	Home Mission Board
26	Sermon on Plan of Salvation
27	Sunday schools, teaching of children
31	Issac Reed III buried in Old Dublin Cemetery, 1908